"This is the most invigorating and enabling book about prayer that I have seen in years! Wry, funny, accessible, wise beyond all appearances, and deeply spiritual, MacBeth warms the soul as well as the heart. So will praying in color."

—Phyllis Tickle, compiler, *The Divine Hours*

"Just as Julia Cameron, in *The Artist's Way*, showed the hardened Harvard businessman he had a creative artist lurking within, MacBeth makes it astonishingly clear that anyone with a box of colors and some paper can have a conversation with God."

—*Publishers Weekly* (starred review)

"Dancer and mathematics instructor MacBeth's charming book may be the first to combine the pleasures of doodling with a discussion of, among other things, lectio divina. Here, she shows how simple drawings—often hardly more than circles and lines with names or ideas or places sketched in and enlivened with color—can focus the praying heart, making prayer something better than a shopping list or a chore and helping the praying believer to carry the wishes and thoughts of the prayer through the day. . . . It is one of the most appealing books on prayer to appear in the last five years. Highly recommended."

—*Library Journal*

"If you saw me at the coffee shop, scribbling away with my colored pencils, you might think I was doodling—and pretty primitive doodling at that. But truth be told, I'm praying—praying in color— learning a new way to talk with God from Sybil MacBeth's unique first book. And it's not just for artists."

—Cindy Crosby, FaithfulReader.com

"This is a book for anyone who has struggled with prayer and who loves color, God, and others enough to try doing it in a new way."

—Alban Institute's *Congregational Resource Guide*

# Praying in
# Black and White

A Hands-on Practice for Men

# Praying in Black and White

SYBIL AND ANDY MACBETH

PARACLETE PRESS

BREWSTER, MASSACHUSETTS

*Praying in Black and White: A Hands-on Practice for Men*

2011 First printing

Library of Congress Cataloging-in-Publication Data
MacBeth, Sybil.
  Praying in black and white : a hands-on practice for men / Sybil and Andy MacBeth.
    p. cm.
  Includes bibliographical references (p.     ).
  ISBN 978-1-55725-809-0 (paperback : alk. paper)
  1.   Christian men—Religious life. 2.     Prayer—Christianity. 3. Doodles—Religious aspects—Christianity.   I. MacBeth, Andrew. II. Title.

  BV4528.2.M25 2011
  248.3'20811--dc23                          2011030256

10 9 8 7 6 5 4 3 2 1

Published by Paraclete Press
Brewster, Massachusetts
www.paracletepress.com
Printed in the United States of America

# CONTENTS

For two very special men in our lives
**—Adam and Conner—**
(WHO HAVE GIVEN US MANY JOYFUL
AND TERRIFYING REASONS TO PRAY)

# 1.
# Prayer Problems and Complaints

Here are some things men say about praying and prayer. If you have any of these problems or have voiced any of these complaints, you are a member of a very large fraternity.

- ❑ I don't know how to pray.

- ❑ What's the purpose of prayer if there are no results?

- ❑ Is there anyone or anything out there listening?

- ❑ Prayer makes me feel stupid.

- ❑ I need to do something concrete rather than just toss words around in my mind or sit or kneel. I can't sit still—and why should I?

- ❑ What's the deal about a *relationship with God?* How can you have a relationship with something or someone you can't see?

❑ What's the point of saying the same prayers over and over again?

❑ I haven't learned any new prayers in years.

❑ I don't know what to say.

❑ My words feel superficial or fake.

❑ My prayers feel like a to-do list for God.

❑ I'm afraid to ask for what I really want.

❑ No one would want to hear what I really feel.

❑ Prayer is boring.

❑ It makes me feel powerless and needy.

# 2.
# Why I Come to the Prayer Table

Andy

Here are some reasons I take the leap into prayer in the first place:

- ❏ I come to prayer because I want to put my life in context, to have some sense of how I fit into the larger scheme of things. Maybe it is arrogant to think I matter this much. But I nourish the hope that God cares about what I do and say and think, and that God is even open to using me as part of whatever God is up to in the world.

- ❏ I come to prayer sometimes because I am feeling anxious or unhappy. Connecting with God makes me feel calmer and more centered.

- ❏ I come to prayer because there are people I care about so much—children, friends, family members—who have huge needs I clearly cannot meet. There must be someone greater than me to share my concern and possibly to aid them in ways I cannot.

❏ I come to prayer out of gratitude. There are moments when I marvel at the gifts I've been given—loving kids, a lively partner, an interesting job, a warm home, a good dinner. None of these things *has* to be. So, great choruses of "thank you" rise up inside me, and I need to say them to someone.

❏ I come to prayer because I care deeply about the world—my country, my neighbors, and the larger world too—and it is such a messed-up place. Bringing a combination of concern, commitment, frustration, and despair to God, I say, "What are you up to?" and ask, "What can I do to help?"

❏ I come to prayer out of habit, and not just habit in the sense of mindlessly repeated behavior. In the ongoing experience of prayer I feel genuinely connected with a life and a power beyond myself. Prayer makes me feel more peaceful, more useful, and more engaged.

❏ I come to prayer with a sense of tempting fate, a sense of risk. It can be like climbing a tall ladder or placing a delicate piece of sculpture on a high shelf. My life feels on the edge. Both excitement and fear well up in me. How might I be pushed or changed or challenged by this encounter?

❏ I come to prayer because it is an anchor for me in a world beyond time and self. In touch with God through prayer, I do not fear death or my own limitations. I feel a part of something good and something beautiful.

❏ I come to prayer because it unites me with other people in a way that is deeper than shared opinions, social events, and even friendship.

❏ I come to prayer for healing at those times when I have been damaged by life's challenges—hurt by criticism, betrayed by a friend, burdened with an aging body, worn down by too much work.

❏ I come to prayer for forgiveness when I have wounded or hurt another person.

# 3.
# What I Bring to the Prayer Table

Andy

I am independent, task-oriented, and goal-focused. I like to see a problem, find a way to fix it, and get the job done. These qualities are among the gifts I have to offer in my work and family life. When it comes to prayer, however, they can be stumbling blocks. Prayer is time spent paying attention to and engaging with a power greater than myself. So, this prayer business is not exactly easy or natural for me. But over the years, I have found a long list of reasons to make the leap, even though my independence and task-orientation work against it. I have discovered that there are forms of prayer that actually take advantage of my natural gifts and turn these potential prayer-inhibitors into assets.

## I am independent and self-sufficient.

My mother and father had a "hold-and-release" philosophy of parenting: "We'll give him roots so that he can grow wings." As an eight-year-old, I rode the bus from the Philadelphia suburb where we lived to the downtown Chester YMCA all by myself. My parents taught me to be independent and self-reliant. They wanted me to grow up and fly away. I learned my lessons well. With my adult wings, I flew a thousand miles away to college with some parental support, a scholarship, and several part-time jobs. I never returned to live in my hometown. By eighteen I had an "I can do it myself" and a "Don't ask for help" attitude.

My wife, Sybil, and I recently drove to the home of a friend in Vermont for the first time. Close to our goal, we realized we had gotten off track and must have missed a turn. While I was turning the car around and preparing to retrace our path, I noticed Sybil doing something it would never have occurred to me to do—calling our host to ask for help. Never mind that this was the quickest way to get straightened out, I was embarrassed. Didn't she know we were competent to do this and could figure it out on our own? It was a challenge we had accepted, and I wanted to see it through to the end. If we had not made the call to our host, we might have wandered through the back roads of Vermont for another hour. We had no idea where we were. Neither we, nor our cell-phone GPS app, knew the difference between River Road and River Street, our final destination. A simple phone call put us back on the right track.

I do not like to look outside of myself for help—from God or anyone else. I know many other men operate this way too. Because of this, we often insist on waiting until some crisis forces us to seek assistance.

## I am task-oriented.

I like to be busy, to engage in physical and mental tasks, work that is world-changing or order-sustaining. On my "day off" I'll mow the lawn, repair a window, and stir-fry vegetables in the wok. A Phillips screwdriver and my bread machine promise challenge and enjoyment for me.

People claim that men are "out of touch" with their feelings and their inner life. Not true. Sometimes we just don't stop long enough to let our insides catch up with our outsides. A group of African tribesmen were once on a journey. At odd intervals they came to a dead stop and stood still. There were no apparent threats and no need of water or a break. When an onlooker asked why they kept doing this, one of the tribesmen replied, "We stop to let our souls catch up with us."

Many of us move so fast and stay so focused on our tasks that we outpace our souls.

## I am goal-focused.

When I take on a task, I have a goal in mind and an outcome I expect. Unfortunately, I live in a world and do a job where outcomes or successes are rarely clear. When my seminary friends and I were still new to parish ministry, one of them expressed his frustration with the lack of clear beginnings and endings in our work. What did success look like in the church? If attendance reached a thousand or a marriage was restored through our counseling, had we done a good job? We might not know for years (or ever!) if our efforts in ministry made a difference to a congregation or its individual members.

My friend decided to go back to school to train as a registered nurse. Today, he feels great satisfaction in his work in the operating room. The restoration of blood flow to a foot during bypass surgery and the removal of a cancerous tumor are successes to which he makes a measurable contribution. Such procedures, with their clear purpose and definite beginning and ending, balance the ambiguity of his ongoing work as a minister in a congregation.

I described my independence, task-orientation, and goal-focus as possible stumbling blocks or impediments to prayer. Fortunately, these can all be turned into equally powerful assets. In the next chapter, we will look at some of the distinctive ways men learn, a first step toward putting these assets to work in learning some practical ways to pray.

# 4.
# How Men Learn

Andy

Generalizations can be incorrect and even dangerous. But, having been a guy for many decades, I've observed and practiced some behaviors and learning strategies common to my gender. Many males find it natural to learn in the following ways:

## 1. We learn from concrete experience.

I loved my ninth-grade biology course because it was the first time I had a class where we spent as much time at the lab table as we did in the lecture hall. When we learned about digestive systems, we actually explored one as we dissected an earthworm. When we were learning about the microbes all around us, we took samples from various surfaces around the school and tried to grow what we found there in our petri dishes. (I remember being really disappointed that the home-ec teacher's counter was completely sterile!)

By ninth grade, I had heard a number of sermons about prayer. But I can't remember a single practical suggestion about how to do it. One thing I could do was help with worship services as an acolyte. I was not a very pious kid, but I liked the fact that there were clear things that I could do during the worship service. At those early Communion services with my minister, Father Redfern, I moved the Gospel book from one side of the altar to the other, and I did it at just the right time. I bowed when the minister bowed. I helped him set the table by passing him first the bread, then the wine, and finally the water. When everything was set, I poured water over his fingers and offered him the carefully folded linen towel—which I arranged on my left wrist, just as I had been taught.

I was clear as could be that God did not care too much about my getting these details right, but I found a certain satisfaction in performing these ritual actions. It was an offering of praise to God. It was something I could do with my hands and my knees, and therefore with my heart as well.

## 2. We learn through physical movement.

Although I did not know it at the time, this is why I got in trouble a lot in kindergarten and first grade. It's also why we may have doodled in our notebooks during college lectures. We need to move, especially when our minds are actively engaged with something. We just seem to absorb things more easily this way. Unfortunately, this can be distracting for other people (such as my first-grade teacher, who wasn't a bad sort, really). In fact, when she would banish me to the hallway, it was just what I needed. I could stretch and walk a few paces, and when I came back in, I'd often absorbed the lesson we had been learning in the classroom a little while before. Moving my body helped my brain take in the learning.

Sybil taught math in a city high school to students who were two years behind their grade level. When she showed them how to do an algebra problem on the board and then asked them to do a similar problem at their desks, they balked. They couldn't focus or concentrate. She finally had the idea to give each student a colored marker and a place at the white board. The switch from sitting and writing on an eight-and-a-half- by eleven-inch piece of paper to standing and writing on a four-foot by eight-foot board was huge. The students could move their whole bodies and write with their whole arms. Drawing six-inch numbers and letters changed their attitudes and their ability to complete the mathematical task.

I maintain that this does not change with age—we just compensate and get sneakier. I'd still rather be at a workbench than a desk—because I can move around there. I can pull a tool off the wall and hold it, even if I have no need to use it right then.

### 3. We learn in groups.

Guys do some of our best learning in groups, but we don't become a group easily. This is why a shared task—like trying to push the opposing football team into the end zone—is so important to us.

After a terrible recent spring ice storm, many trees were down on the mountain where my mother lives. Driveways were blocked and devastation was everywhere. Once the road crews and professional tree people had come through and done their work, great piles of branches remained at every turn in the road. One weekend, a guy who lives at the bottom of the mountain arranged to rent a big chipper, hooked it to his pickup, and invited his neighbors to help do something with all the brush. Ten guys worked like dogs for the 36 hours they had rented the expensive machine. When they were done, not only did the mountain look better but also the men of the mountain had built a far closer bond than they had before. They can't wait for their next project.

What is it that makes groups helpful? I appreciate the wisdom and encouragement of guys who are older or more experienced than I, and I enjoy the chance to share what I've learned with others. I also appreciate the playfulness that a group can bring out in me. I value the guys I can laugh with if my experiment fails, or who egg me on when I'm not quite sure I'm ready to take up tennis again. Most of all, I enjoy having a shared task to tackle. I would rather get out on the tennis court with three other guys and let them give me some pointers than spend an hour with a coach.

The puzzling but potentially life-giving practice of prayer is definitely a task worth taking on together.

An individual can practice most of the prayer methods suggested in this book, but learning them with a group can give us an ongoing network for encouragement and accountability. In the same way recovering alcoholics and addicts stay clean and sober by sharing their "strength, hope, and experience," men on a quest for a deeper experience of prayer can be a bloc of support for each other. Jesus knew this too. He began his public life looking for colleagues, for comrades, for disciples who could share in the enormous work he was up to in the world. From his position as a small-town guy from a not-so-important country, he invited others to help him make a difference for their neighbors.

# 5.
# Prayer in the Bible

The Bible doesn't offer much instruction about prayer or technique for doing it. It just says "Pray." Examples of the word *pray* are scattered throughout the Old Testament. Here "Pray" does not necessarily indicate a spiritual act. "Pray" means to petition, ask, or plead. It was and sometimes is used in common conversation. "I pray you don't spend all of your money at the casino." In Genesis 12, Abram and Sarai are about to encounter the Egyptians. Abram says to his wife, Sarai, "Say, I pray thee, thou art my sister: that it may be well with me for thy sake" (KJV). In more contemporary words of this passage, Abram might say, "Please, pretty please, Sarah, pretend you're my sister instead of my wife. You can spend some time in the court and then they won't kill me."

Abram or Abraham, as he is later called, not only "prayed" to Sarai, he prayed to God. He is possibly the first person in the Bible to petition God directly. Genesis 20:17 says, "So Abraham prayed unto God:

and God healed Abimelech, and his wife, and his maidservants; and they bare children" (KJV). But how he prayed to God is a mystery. Did he use words like he did with Sarai? Did he stand up, sit down, or run in circles? No details of his prayer technique are available.

In the New Testament Gospel of Matthew, chapter 6, Jesus gives us all kinds of "don'ts" about prayer.

1. Don't pray where you can be seen and admired for your piety like the hypocrites. Go into a closet or a hiding place or your room where no one but God can see and hear you.

2. Don't babble lots of words like the pagans. Don't try to impress God. God already knows what you need.

Even here, we don't know if the hypocrites and pagans were shouting out loud or carrying signs. Were they groveling in the dirt or turning cartwheels while they uttered endless streams of words?

The one concrete example we have of prayer instruction in all of Scripture is what Christians call the Lord's Prayer. In Matthew 6:9–15 (NIV) Jesus says to the disciples,

*This, then, is how you should pray: "Our Father in heaven, hallowed be your name, your kingdom come, your will be done on earth as it is in heaven. Give us today our daily bread. And forgive us our debts, as we also have forgiven our debtors. And lead us not into temptation, but deliver us from the evil one." For if you forgive other people when they sin against you, your heavenly Father will also forgive you. But if you do not forgive others their sins, your Father will not forgive your sins.*

When Jesus says, "This, then, is how you should pray," what exactly does he mean? Is this the only prayer we're ever supposed to say? Or was he modeling the kinds of things we pray for—God's will, daily sustenance, forgiveness, and so on—and the respect with which we do it? Dozens of books about the Lord's Prayer exist.

The bottom line is this: The Bible does not provide a complete instruction guide for how to pray. So if you are not entirely clear about how to pray, you have lots of company.

# 6.
# A New Experience of Prayer

Sybil

I can't remember a time when I didn't pray. My mother injected me with prayers and prayer-talk from the time I was old enough to listen and speak. But most of the prayers I said were precrafted ones. I memorized psalms and recited them out loud and to myself. They gave me comfort and further saturated me with a belief in God. I prayed the rote prayers of my tradition alone and in a worship setting with other people. Prayer for me was the affirmation of church beliefs about God and the recitation of the words of my spiritual ancestors. It was a way to honor and revere the One who made me and loved me. A list of "Thank-yous" might also have been in the mix.

But having a heart-to-heart conversation with God was not really in my repertoire. My prayers were not personal communication with a friend.

As an adult and the spouse of Andy, I met people of diverse faith traditions and denominations. I listened to preachers, priests, speakers, and laypeople pray elegant extemporaneous words—words of love and affection, words of adoration, words of need and hunger, words of sorrow and despair. In some ways I was mesmerized by their skill but also embarrassed. This kind of sharing was way more personal than I had ever been with God—or probably anyone else for that matter. Unlike many of my female friends, I was not very adept at sentimental or emotional expression. Quadratic equations and basketball plays were far more comfortable topics of conversation. Feelings were something I neither recognized easily in myself nor shared with others when I did—let alone with the Creator. Hearing the honest prayers of others granted me the permission to expand my emotional vocabulary and openness with God.

To this day, however, prayers with words do not flow from my mouth, heart, or mind with much ease. There is irony for me in this impairment, because I love words. I love the meanings, origins, and nuances of words. Their physical appearance and their composition intrigue me. Scrabble® is my favorite game. A day without computer Scrabble® is like being grounded for a week.

As much as I love words, they often betray me. When I need them most they vanish. In conversation with people or with God, words disappear, leaving me blathering and flustered. Like little cowards, they scamper behind me and only reappear when the need or the poignancy of the moment is over. Sometimes the only words that come out of my mouth in conversation are "Really," "Uh huh," "Wow. . . ." Not exactly profound responses or conversation boosters. "Thank you," "O God," "Help," and "#!*+," . . . tumble out in my awkward prayers. I'm sure God is okay with those primitive cheers and cries, but I am left feeling unsatisfied and stupid.

Besides my problem with words, I have a short attention span and a chronic need to move. Daydreaming and fidgetiness are not usually held up as the qualities of a crackerjack prayer warrior.

My inadequacy in prayer reached its peak several years ago. In a single year, six or seven close friends and family members were diagnosed with a variety of vicious and life-threatening forms of cancer. I prayed for them. I prayed for them in the way one of my friends calls "passionate begging." "Please, God, heal them." "Let them live to see their children graduate from high school." "Release them from pain." After a while I was sick of my own pathetic words. Why couldn't I say eloquent prayers for healing and care like the people I admired? My words felt childish and inadequate. They felt demanding and desperate. I could think of nothing new to say. And I wasn't sure God even cared about my pleas. How many times would I have to speak these words in order for God to do what I wanted? What was the point of the prayers if my friends weren't going to get well?

One morning, during the illness of my friends, I toted my black pen and colored markers to the screened-in porch. I sat down at the table and started to doodle. When I say doodle, I mean that. My drawings did not look like anything in real life. Doodling is a form of relaxation for me. It's mindless, but active and fun. I'm not an artist. I bear huge shame about my lack of visual artistic skill. My mother and grandmothers, both artists and both Sybils, did not bequeath their ability for drawing, painting, and sculpture to me.

I drew an amoeba, my favorite shape. I added lines and dots. I added color. I wrote the name "Sue" inside the shape. Sue, my sister-in-law, was one of the people I was praying for. She was forty-seven, had two children in high school, and had stage-four lung cancer. Writing her name in the drawing was unconscious. I continued to draw and to focus on her name.

At the end of the drawing, I noticed I had been quiet for at least ten minutes. My worry for Sue was less. And then I realized I had prayed. There were no words, but a handing over of Sue into God's care. It was as if we were quietly sitting in a room together—God, Sue, and I—just being there, holding each other in love. What I needed to do in prayer was spend time with God and spend time with Sue. I didn't necessarily have words, and God didn't need me to have the words. The doodling created something for my hands to do and my eyes to watch while I became still enough on the inside to recognize the presence of God.

After I drew the doodle for Sue, I prayed for the other friends on my prayer list in the same way: I drew, focused on the person, and allowed the movement of my hand to take me to a place of inner stillness where God could break through to my antsy and attention-deprived self.

Not only did the doodling give me a time of quiet and stillness, but also it gave me a visual prayer list. The act of drawing the doodles planted a pictorial image in my brain. Throughout the day the drawing would pop back into my head and prompt me to pray. When it did, either I could pray a verbal prayer for each person or I could be quiet for a few moments and offer each person into God's care without words.

In marketing terms, I now had a process and a product. The process was the time of quiet with God while I drew and focused on my friends. The product was the visual hard copy of the prayer.

This way of praying was a huge epiphany for me, the beginning of a new kind of prayer practice. *Praying in color*, as I nicknamed it, did not try to get rid of my weaknesses in prayer; it endorsed them. It took my inability to draw or to find words or to sit still and gave me a way to pray. My needs as a kinesthetic and visual learner were addressed as I drew and watched the images on the page. I call *praying in color* my 2 Corinthians 12 prayer form: "My grace is sufficient for you, for my power is made perfect in weakness" (2 Cor. 12:9, NIV). My expertise was unnecessary for prayer; my weaknesses were.

# 7.
# Tools for Prayer

The tools you will need to try this way of praying are simple:

1. A piece of paper
2. A pen

## The Paper
The paper can be anything larger than a postage stamp—a Post-It, an index card, an eight-and-a-half- by eleven-inch piece of computer paper, whatever you can find. . . . The back of an old envelope from the trash will work in a pinch.

## The Pen
A roller-ball or gel pen creates a smoother line than a ballpoint.

Beyond the paper and pen you will need a vocabulary of doodling and a name for God.

## Doodling

In case you haven't doodled since elementary school or never did, here is a mini doodling lesson.

## Draw:

*Lines*    *Circles*    *Triangle*    *Ellipses*

*Squares or Rectangles*    *Figure Eights*    *Dots*

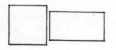  

*Regular Polygons*    *Irregular Polygons*    *Amoebas*

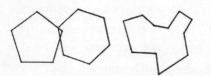

*Spirals*  *Wavy Lines*  *Zigzags*

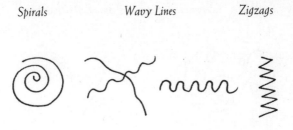

*Arcs*  *Scribbles*

Combine some of the above shapes and strokes together:

*Polygons with Arcs*  *Self-Repeating Shapes*  *Triangles with Circles*

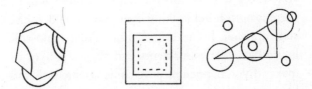

*Scribbles with Squares*       *Figure Eights with Lines*

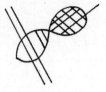

*Amoebas with Dots*

The point of showing these options is just to give you permission to draw whatever you want. These are suggestions of where to start. Let your hand take you where it wants on the page. In other words, there is no teacher looking over your shoulder. Just start drawing. It can even be ugly. Your hand will figure out what movements and shapes it likes to make. If you happen to have some artistic skill and like realism, go ahead and draw boats, stop signs, trees, or whatever.

## Names for God

If you are a person who prays already, you probably have a way you start your prayers: "Our Father," "Holy One," "Dear God. . . ." The ways we address God are endless. Many of us use the same name for God all of the time—the one we learned as a kid or the one we chose when we became serious about our spiritual life. But in case you're unsatisfied with the name you use or just want to stretch your understanding of the infinite facets of God, here are some ideas.

**Jesus**   *Holy Spirit*

**God**   Healer   **Savior**   Creator

**father**   Abba   **Redeemer**

YAHWEH  **Lord**  *Father-Mother God*

We can add adjectives to the above names:

**LOVING GOD**  Brother Jesus

*Healing Savior*  *Higher Power*

**Forgiving Lord**  ALMIGHTY FATHER

Different denominations and religions have traditions about the names they use in prayer.

Catholics might use any of the names above but also pray to *Mary* or to one of the saints like **Anthony.**

Jews might not write the unspeakable name of God, but use **G-d**, **Elohim**, or **Adonai**.

With some doodling vocabulary and some God names, you are ready to begin. Grab some paper and a pen and pray.

# 8.
# Praying in Black and White

Choose the name for God you want to use first.
Write the name in the middle of the page or near
the top of the page. Draw around it—simple strokes
and shapes. Writing the name announces this as a
time apart with God.

While you are drawing, imagine you are sitting
with a friend or someone you respect. You listen
and allow your friend to speak without interruption,

without butting in or thinking of what you will say next. If your friend doesn't speak and you have something to say, say it. But words are not necessary. Resist the temptation to leave the room or to speak just for the sake of speaking. Just think of this as a chance to spend some quiet together-time with your friend—in this case God.

Continue to draw and to focus your attention on the name you choose. Say it to yourself if you want. What you are doing is creating a space and time for God to visit with you and you to visit God. Drawing can keep your hands and body busy if you are uncomfortable with the silence. It is an active way to tell the rest of your body that it's okay to be right here right now. Prayer is not just a head thing, but also an activity of the whole body and the whole self.

If words come easily to you in prayer, let them fly. But when the words run out, keep praying without them. Just draw, focus on God's name, and listen. You won't necessarily hear anything. But think of this as a time of stillness. In Psalm 46:10 (NIV), God says, "Be still, and know that I am God."

people. So it is with God. Whether our relationship with God is old or new, it's important to have time with God. Since words in prayer often vanish for me, I can't always guarantee "quality" time with God. So to build my relationship, I need lots of "quantity" time—even if the quantity is just bits and snatches during the day. I need to create time with God— lots of meetings, whether long or short. Those little increments of time build a relationship.

# 9.
# Praying for Others

Sybil

Praying for others is called intercessory prayer. When we "intercede" we ask God to be involved in the lives of the people we are praying for—for healing, for safety, for a change of direction, for support. . . . The words for these prayers are not always easy to find. When this frustrates you, create a prayer drawing instead. This is a way you can spend time with the people you want to pray for and offer them into God's care.

☐ Mark the start of your prayer time by taking a deep breath and releasing it. Inhale and exhale with equal strength.

☐ Begin at the top or in the middle of the page as described in chapter 7. Ask God to be present as you pray. Use words or just the strokes and movements of your pen.

☐ When you come to a stop, take a deep breath and release a deep exhale.

☐ Say a line from Scripture like:

"You strengthen me more and more; you enfold and comfort me." Psalm 71:21 (BCP) or "Our soul waits for the LORD; he is our help and shield." Psalm 33:20 (NRSV)

☐ Whenever you're ready, move to a different place on the page. Draw a new shape or design. Write the name of a person for whom you want to pray in or near the design. Focus your attention on the name of the person. Keep your hand moving by adding lines, dots, arcs, shapes. . . . Go back to chapter 7 for ideas if you get stuck. Release the person into God's care. Don't fight for words.

☐ When you complete the drawing for this person, take a deep breath and release it.

☐ Say the line of Scripture you chose before. Repeat this each time you finish praying for a person. The breath and the words of Scripture are a way to release any concern and worry you still have. They also create a space between the person you just prayed for and the next person you add to the page.

☐ Pray for another person. Find a space and shape for their name. Repeat the process of drawing and praying. Add details with your pen.

☐ Draw a prayer for everyone on your list. Besides people, you can pray for your city, your country, and any issue of concern to you.

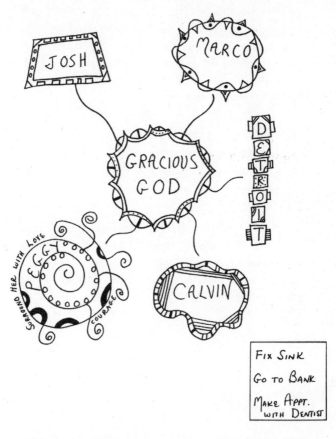

- If words come to you, pray them. Feel free to write them on the drawing.
- If recurring distractions interrupt while you are praying, create a box for them on the bottom of the page. Write yourself a note so you can let go of the

distraction and continue to pray. Or if a distraction feels urgent, make it part of your prayer. When you finish praying and drawing, sit with the page in front of you. Let the names and images soak into your mind. Spend another moment with each person in silence or say a simple prayer or "Amen."

Place the drawing where you can see it during the day—perhaps on the refrigerator or in your car. When you notice it again or when the image pops into your head, offer a quick prayer.

❏ Remember, praying in black and white is not about creating great art. It's about praying in a way that relies less on words and spending time with God in an active, visual way. It's about praying even when you have nothing to say.

# 10.
# Barriers to Prayer

Andy

## Being a Novice Again

Many of us have worked hard to gain competence in our profession, to achieve certification, tenure, partner status, whatever our work demands. How do we get comfortable being a novice again—being a learner or beginner—being "under construction"—if this is what it takes to pray effectively?

I have a friend who has modeled for me the way of the novice. Sally taught dance at New York University and performed as a soloist and corps member of several dance companies. The irony of her dance career is that Sally had polio as a child. It was not a huge disability for her, but weakness in her left leg was always an issue. Sally knew she wanted to dance and did not say, "Oh, I could never do that." She wanted to dance, so she was willing to dance poorly for a while. And because she was willing to start as an incompetent student, she became a skilled one.

At the age of 58, Sally decided she wanted to learn to draw and paint. Post-polio syndrome has left her dominant right hand with a chronic shake. She can barely sign her name. But the desire to paint was stronger than her physical limiations. She started drawing with her left hand. She took a calligraphy class and spent hours learning to make marks and strokes with the use of her untrained hand. When she advanced to drawing classes, she begged her teachers for correction and guidance. In the ten years since Sally began the journey with a calligraphy pen, she has become an artist. Her detailed and accurate botanical drawings have been shown in and won medals from exhibitions by the Royal Horticultural Society in London and the American Society of Botanical Artists in New York. Sally has the humility of a chronic novice, but now she has the skill of an expert.

It has been helpful to me to remember how much fun it can be to learn something new. A few years ago, I took up fly-fishing. I was experienced with a spinning reel, but I knew nothing about this. I felt like a six-year-old as I practiced casting in an empty parking lot. I loved it. The first time I got to cast in a river and the first time I saw a fish rise to take a fly I had presented ever-so-carefully were magic moments. Being a novice can be fun. One of these days, I'm going to learn to play golf. I'll take some lessons, get advice from friends, and just enjoy the new venture. I want to be like Sally. Not because she has become an expert, but because she enjoys the process, the journey of learning something new.

It may be that being a prayer novice is hard for us because we assume that everybody else already knows how to pray and has years of experience. This is far from the truth. Whatever the case may have been back in history, many people of faith today grow to adulthood having received very little coaching about prayer. If this is you, you are not alone!

I have also found it helpful to remember how potentially important prayer is. With a twist on a popular saying, a pastor friend says, "If something is really worth doing, it's worth doing poorly." Prayer is important enough that I want to learn what I can and do what I can—even if it's clear that I'll never be a pro. Being even a pretty-good pray-er would be fantastic. If I can pray well enough to someday share what I know with my kids or grandkids, then who cares if I am a prayer expert?

## Actually Believing—or Not

Another barrier to prayer could be that honestly, deep in your heart of hearts, you are not so sure if you believe in God. Or, if you do believe, you are not sure what you think God is like. It is no insult to God to take your questionings and uncertainty seriously. In fact, doing so recognizes that faith is too important for anything less than total honesty.

As a pastor of many years, I can tell you that few people's faith is always deep and certain. The ups and downs of life and changes in our own mood can have a dramatic effect on our ability to believe. My own experience is this—you can go ahead and pray in a way that says, "God, if you are there, hear me. Please let me know that you are present and that you are real."

At times, it may be helpful to not even use the word *God*. As some people do at Twelve-Step or AA meetings, just think of God as your "higher power," whatever that is. If there are values bigger than you, ideals you ascribe to, hopes that override everything else, let that be the object of your prayer for now.

You might also like to consider offering prayers to Jesus. Although this may sound very pious, it could really be noncommittal. We know Jesus first of all (as his disciples did!) as one who shares our humanity—our hopes and disappointments, relationships and betrayals, great days and hard ones.

Walk with Jesus for a while; share your perceptions and emotions with him; let him share some insights with you. Whether or not you ultimately come to think of him as the one in whom God is supremely present in this world is just between you and Jesus. For now just think of him as a friend, someone who can comprehend what it is like to be you.

## Drawing? Are You Kidding?

A final barrier to what we call praying in black and white is fear: "I can't draw. I don't want to draw. Don't ask me to try."

Try and let all of this go. This prayer form has nothing to do with art. (In fact, artistically gifted people can get distracted from prayer if they get too caught up in the effort to create a beautiful work of art.) Think of this as a way to keep your hands busy, to stay focused on God, and to create a tangible, visible reminder of your prayer concerns that may be useful as the day or week goes on.

Your drawings don't have to be for display. In fact, while some people may find it helpful to look over their prayer drawings or post them in a private place, many of us never look at our work again. The One who needs to see it already has.

# 11.
# Keeping It Practical and Concrete

Andy

Even though I am a highly intuitive person, this guy feels a strong need to produce something each day, to have concrete results from my daily work. Because this does not always happen on the job, I spend a fair bit of my free time working on our drafty old 1912 house—caulking a window or rewiring a chandelier. And in some funny way this feeds me. I feel the same need for concreteness in my relationship with God.

I have found a variety of ways to make my prayers tangible.

## Praying at My Desk

I take advantage of whatever tools are on my desk when I do my daily prayers. I have an elegant fifteen-inch ruler, aluminum with a cork backing. I don't remember why I bought it, but it makes great, smooth lines. When I want to pray with straight lines, I use the ruler to create a grid, a square, or a starburst of straight lines all connected to the same starting point. It has an orderly, geometric feel, even if my life and my prayers feel chaotic. I also have a compass and a protractor, tools leftover from ninth grade. Being able to create an almost-perfect circle in my prayer drawings can be very satisfying. See what you can do with multiple circles. Sometimes each person I am praying for ends up in a circle. At other times, I might use dozens of circles just to focus my prayer energy on one person and their needs.

Different kinds of paper can also be useful.

Beautiful journals (the kind you might find in a museum gift shop) used to scare the pudding out of me. They were nice to hold and behold, but I could never imagine myself writing in one. Such journals are perfect for prayer with a pen, however, so I suggest you pull one off the bookshelf (we have about a half dozen given to us as gifts) and give it a try.

Graph paper is also a great resource. I have prayed on individual sheets of graph paper, but I also have one of those black and white "marble" composition books with graph paper inside—the kind you may have used in high school or college. They also come with lined paper or plain paper, but there is something comforting for me about the graph paper. I'm more adventurous with it than I am on plain paper. One of the big surprises for me was that sometimes my pen-prayers were not just shapes with square corners. Curved lines and circles sometimes emerge from the tiny squares!

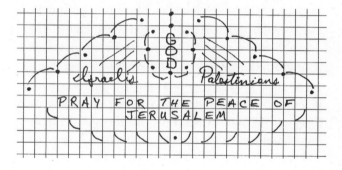

Many different companies send me paper calendars each year, usually with a separate page for each month. They tend to be composed of one- to two-inch squares. I have found that these are perfect guides for my intercessions. I can put a person-of-the-day on the calendar each morning, with a name and appropriate decoration, or I can do a whole week's worth of names (so I don't forget anyone) and add my doodles later as I pray for them on their day. Other concerns work well here too. I can pray my way through Africa or the European Union. Or I can devote a week to the president, members of Congress, the governor, and the mayor. I can't think of anyone who needs more prayer attention than my city council—and I am better off not trying to pray for them in words. I just lift them up to God one at a time.

| WEDNESDAY | THURSDAY | FRIDAY | SATURDAY |
|---|---|---|---|
| New Moon **1** <br> Clara & Mae | Conner **2** | Don + Anne **3** | **4** <br> PRESIDENT |
| **8** | First Quarter **9** | **10** | **11** |
| Full Moon **15** | **16** | **17** | **18** |
| **22** | Last Quarter **23** | **24** | **25** |
| **29** | **30** | | |

A journal, graph paper, notebook, computer paper, an envelope, a business card. . . . All of this comes down to the slogan my wife and I sometimes say aloud: "Have paper will pray."

## Paperless Prayers

Praying on the computer is not as crazy as it sounds. Think of all the time that people spend on games like computer solitaire. What are these but ways to kill time? Try devoting a few minutes of screen time each day to prayer. Many drawing programs and applications provide an easy way to draw. Use the shape menus to create circles and polygons. Add lines and other designs. The process of adding shapes and names on the computer can be as meditative as drawing by hand.

One advantage of making a prayer drawing on the computer is its lasting presence in front of me on the screen. After I have prayed this way, I can make the drawing my screen saver, minimize it to look at later, or send it via e-mail or text message to others to initiate a virtual prayer chain.

Doodling apps abound on smart phones too. Try downloading one and see if you can pray on your phone, anywhere, anytime.

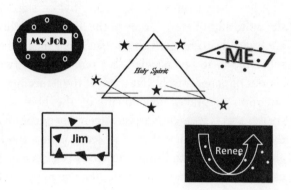

## Praying Your To-Do List

Most mornings I wake up with a "to-do" list bouncing around my brain. I keep a notepad next to my bed where I write things I need to remember. The list often begins to take shape before I go to sleep the night before. Some of the items on the list are just tasks to be performed—such as a magazine subscription to be canceled or a reminder that we are out of paper towels. But some of the items merit attention in prayer. The board of the homeless shelter that is struggling to stay open, my upcoming counseling session with a troubled couple—these are things I want to bring into God's presence and care. Sometimes I add the to-do items to my prayer page, mixing them right in with the other people and concerns I am praying about. Another option is to give my day's to-do list a whole page of its own. I jot down a word or two that will help me remember each major concern. Then I pray around it with pen or pencil for a minute or two before I go to the next item and the next.

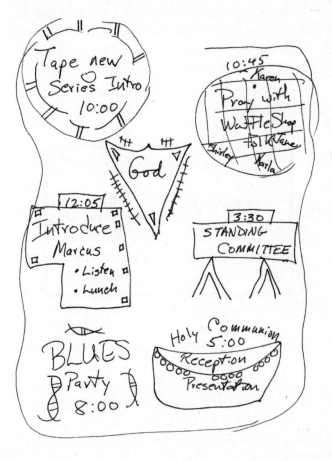

Sometimes, my to-do list has had to be jotted onto the back of a business card. If I have a short list or one *major* item to remember, this works really well. I write a word or two, then take a moment to add some lines or shapes that reflect how it went or how I hope it will go.

I take comfort from knowing that Jesus' original disciples were also always on the lookout for ways to make their prayer concrete. Sometimes their clumsy efforts may have even provided the whole group with a good laugh. Remember the story of Jesus going up on what came to be known as the "Mount of the Transfiguration" with Peter, James, and John? The three of them had a vision of Jesus talking with two other great men of faith—Moses and Elijah—and Peter blurted out this offer: "Lord, how about if we build three shrines (or tents), one for you, one for Moses, and one for Elijah?" Peter's immediate impulse was to want to convert this momentary vision into something permanent—a building! He and his companions did not get to do this, and as they came down from the mountain, Jesus told them to keep the experience to themselves for now. I have a hunch that Peter picked up a rock as he came down that path and kept it in his pocket as a tangible reminder of what he had seen.

# 12.
# Praying Scripture—
# *Lectio Divina*

Sybil

Analyzing, studying, interpreting, memorizing, reading, reciting . . . are all ways I engage the words of the Bible. But praying the Scriptures using an ancient Christian practice called *lectio divina* has transformed my relationship with the Bible and with God. In English, the Latin words *lectio divina* mean "divine" or "sacred reading."

*Lectio divina* is not historical study or critical analysis of a biblical text. It is a way to pray the Scriptures and to listen for the voice of God speaking to me at a particular moment in time. If Scripture is truly the *Living Word*, it will speak to me in new ways every day. In *lectio divina*, I ask God to speak the truth I need to hear.

*Lectio divina* is a four-part prayer form:

❑ *Lectio* means "to read."

❑ *Meditatio* means "to meditate."

❏ *Oratio* means "to speak or pray."

❏ *Contemplatio* means "to contemplate."

Many of the teachings and books about *lectio divina* encourage sitting in a chair with a straight spine and upturned hands in the lap. This kind of stillness is agony for me. My hybrid version will give you permission to move. So gather your pen and paper and prepare a place to pray.

## Lectio

Choose a single line of Scripture. Select one that will be read in worship on Sunday or one that intrigues you. In a jam, open the Bible and point to a sentence. Here is an example:

> *You have fed them with the bread of tears; you have given them bowls of tears to drink. Psalm 80:5 (BCP)*

Write the passage on a piece of paper. Write it large enough so you can really see it. Read it slowly. Read it five or ten times. Read it aloud if possible. Ask God to give you a word for the day. Read the passage over and over again until a word jumps out at you. When you have the word, circle it. (If no particular word cries out, just choose one at random.)

YOU HAVE FED THEM
WITH THE (BREAD) OF
TEARS; YOU HAVE
GIVEN THEM BOWLS
OF TEARS TO DRINK.

I chose the word *bread*. It is the word I will use for the rest of the prayer. In the next two sections I will ask God to speak to me through this word.

## Meditatio

*Meditatio* means to "meditate, chew on, or mull over." My favorite definition is "marinate." I will take the word *bread* and marinate in it. I will let it soak into my pores and listen for what it might have to say to me. I like to do this in two ways. You might try doing it on another piece of paper too.

❑ In the middle of a clean piece of paper, write the word you chose. Now write down everything you know about this word. Brainstorm; do a brain or data dump. Write down anything that comes to mind, even if it seems silly or far-fetched. What we're doing is clearing our minds of any preconceptions or thoughts we already have about the word. Some people call this *webbing* or *mind-mapping*.[1] You can quit when you've exhausted your ideas. You can also set a timer for three to five minutes and create a time boundary on your brainstorm.

❑ Now take a new piece of paper. Write your word
  again in the middle of the page. This time don't
  think about the word. Instead of teasing ideas out
  of your brain, listen to the word. Pretend it is a
  guest in your house. Let it speak to you. Listen
  for what God might say to you through the word.
  While you are listening, draw. Doodle around the
  word in the same way described in chapter 8. Let
  the movement of the hand help you focus on the
  word and release anxiety. Get still on the inside
  by moving on the outside. If you hear other things
  about the word, write them down. If the thoughts
  and words from the previous brain dump come
  back to you, write them down again. Use a timer
  or stop when you feel finished.

## Oratio

*Oratio* means "to speak or to pray." In this part of
*lectio divina*, we talk to God in the more traditional
way of prayer. This is a chance to use words and have
a conversation with God. We can ask God about the
word we've been sitting with for the past ten minutes.
"What do you want me to hear and learn from this
word? Why is this word important today?"

Some practitioners of *lectio divina* use this time as a
chance to express feelings to God. For some of us this
is awkward. I'm not very good at verbal expressions

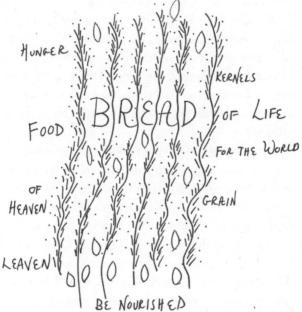

of intimacy. I have trouble saying "I love you" even to the people I love. I'm shy with words of tenderness and care. Saying words of love and adoration to God is no less embarrassing. Maybe at the very least, we can be silent and imagine God loving us.

You can also see this time as a conversation with Jesus. I have friends who like to imagine Jesus sitting on a rock; they are chatting face-to-face. The face-to-face conversation seems way too scary to me. So I've imagined myself sitting back-to-back on a park bench with Jesus. It feels friendly, but not too intimate.

Even though this step is about oral conversation, I like to have my pen in hand. It can act as a little buffer between God and my shyness. Whether you're comfortable or not with this talking-to-God stuff, let your feelings and questions come to the surface. Write down your thoughts and questions: "Help my unbelief." "I'd like to know you better." "Open my heart." "Why this word, God?" While you talk and write, continue to draw. Drawing during this step helps me to focus and to listen. Writing helps me to see what I'm thinking and feeling. I might not "hear" anything, but creating this time and space for conversation with God prepares the soil of my heart for a response when it does come.

Take two to five minutes (or longer) with this step.

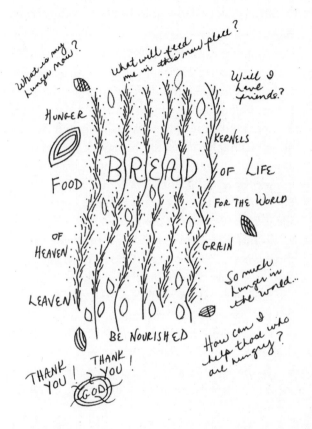

## Contemplatio

This is the last step of *lectio divina*. I think of this
step as the rest stop or the cool-down period before
I go about the normal business of my life. *Contemplatio*
is the step where I release the word I have chosen
and all of the thoughts and feelings about the word.
I give up all of the activity of drawing, thinking, and
writing. I close my eyes, still my mind, and imagine
myself falling into the huge hammock of God. Even
as normally fidgety as I am, I'm ready for a couple of
minutes of rest after the work of the previous steps.
Being held by God feels like a pretty good way to
spend a few minutes of my day.

So put down your pen. Set a timer for two to
three minutes. Sit in a chair or lie on the floor. Close
your eyes. Take a deep breath and release it. Stay in
the moment. Let go of the past ten minutes; don't
think of the next ten. Breathe.

Some people have huge spiritual "ahas" during
this time. A new revelation about the chosen word
breaks through the silence. Transformation happens
for them. Other people just enjoy the rest and the
quiet time.

My time with *lectio divina* never feels wasted.
At the very least, I know more about the word
I chose than ever before. And I never hear the
word in exactly the same way again. During the
*meditatio* I teased a lot of associations from my brain.

I marinated in the word and listened to it. A week or a month later, it might come back to me with new relevance or insight.

Occasionally, I have a spiritual breakthrough. One time I read the Scripture verse I had chosen for a large group retreat. No word or words jumped out at me. Almost as a joke I picked three words: *but*, *no*, and *so*—not exactly meaty, spiritual concepts. I went through the four steps of *lectio divina*. A week after the retreat, those three words popped into my head and said, "You use us when you want to feel smart or superior. You keep your distance from other people with us." I saw myself with crossed arms and a haughty look, "*But* have you thought of this option?" Or, "*No*, that won't do." Or, "*So* what?" It was not a pretty picture. But I knew it was true, at least sometimes. God had spoken to me through those three little words and told me something I needed to hear.

People ask, "Doesn't *lectio divina* take Scripture out of context?" My response is, "Yes." But that's not the point. *Lectio divina* is not the study of Scripture. It uses Scripture as a way to initiate a conversation with God. It only takes a single word to deepen our relationship and experience God's abundant and abiding love.

# 13.
# Breath Prayer

Andy

"Forgiving God, change my life." "Holy Spirit, give me confidence today." "Jesus, help me." These one-liners are the honest prayers we blurt out in unconscious moments of despair or gratitude. They are so short, they almost feel like non-prayers. But these little bytes of communication with God can become the kernels for a way to pray called *breath prayer*.[2]

The classic breath prayer is the Jesus Prayer from the sixth century: "Lord Jesus Christ, Son of God, have mercy on me, a sinner." The prayer includes *a "name"*: "Lord Jesus Christ, Son of God" and *a "request"*: "have mercy on me, a sinner."

The purpose of a breath prayer is to have a way to stay in constant communication with God, to "pray unceasingly," as 1 Thessalonians 5:17 says. By repeating the words of the prayer over and over again, we find they become as natural and unconscious as our breath. One way to start this practice is to write out a breath prayer and draw around it until it feels familiar and natural. You can use the tools of *Praying in Black and White* to do this.

Start with a simpler version of the Jesus Prayer: "Lord Jesus Christ, have mercy on me." Take out your pen and paper, but before you even begin to write, repeat the prayer slowly. Say it in sync with your breathing, if that seems helpful. Try "Lord Jesus Christ" on the inhale, and "have mercy on me" with the exhale. If breathing in sync feels complicated, just say the words at your own pace.

Now begin to write . . . and to draw. Write the words of the prayer—once or many times—and begin to draw around them. Let the doodling help you keep the words coming. Let the words move from being sounds you make with your lips to being words that come from your heart and lungs, from the very center of your being. If your pen stops moving at some point but the prayer continues, that's okay. If the prayer stops, use the movement of your pen on the paper to get it going again. Having a drawing of your breath prayer, especially when it is new, helps reinforce its power in our imagination.

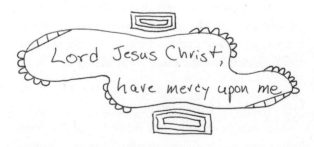

I sometimes start my day with a breath prayer. I say and draw the prayer; other times I sit quietly in a chair and say it. When I practice a breath prayer like this, I find it helpful to set a timer for five, ten, or fifteen minutes. Constantly checking my watch is a distraction. Many computers and cell phones have timers, but an old-fashioned kitchen timer works well too. The use of a breath prayer has often been referred to as "unceasing prayer." When I am using the prayer daily, it becomes part of me. At certain moments during the day I get the sense that the prayer is still going, still part of my breathing, even when I am not consciously thinking it.

Even after I was ordained, I remained the sort of believer who would tell you, "I'm betting my life on God, that God is real and that God cares. But there is no way you can always *know* for certain that God is there." Praying a breath prayer changed that for me and gave me the gift of moments when I knew in some deep way that God was as present with me as my friends and the chair I was sitting in.

## Finding Your Own Prayer

My own prayer practice involves not the Jesus Prayer but another more personal breath prayer—one that I would say God has given me, a prayer that expresses my faith and my need at this time. God will give you one too.

In order to get started, select a name for God, the *praise* part of the prayer. It could be a familiar name or one that is a little bit of a stretch for you. Do you have a hunch about what name for God you should use? Trust that God will help you find the right name and that you will know if you're using one that's not quite right for you now. Write it on your paper and draw something simple around it.

Now create the petition you will pair with it. Keep it simple. There are lots of things we could pray for, but what is the thing that would meet your deepest need? What do you *most need* from God? My first breath prayer was:

Lord Jesus, let me feel your peace.

This may have been just right for me because I was a pretty anxious young man. Once the prayer took shape, I probably prayed it for about three years, until one day I realized that I *did* feel the Lord's peace in a pretty consistent way. I was ready for a new prayer!

Don't worry too much about getting the words exactly right. My experience is that if they are not exactly the prayer you need to be praying, they will change over the first days or weeks. In most cases, the prayer really needs to be *for you*. If there is someone in your life whose needs are overwhelming right now, what do *you* need in order to be most supportive of them?

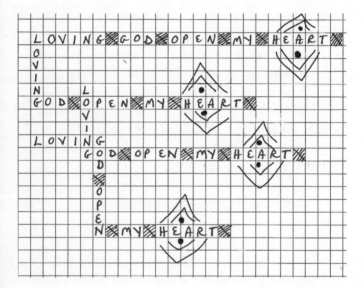

Once you and God have settled on your own breath prayer, let it become part of you. Say it at traffic lights and in the elevator. Write and draw it when you are at your desk or your computer. Pray it instead of obsessing about some past or future event. Let your breath prayer be the words you say in your head, instead of the regrettable words you want to say aloud.

# 14.
# Praying with Others

Andy

Men praying together can be a powerful force. All we lack in most cases is an initiator, someone who will bring us together and give us a framework for action. There are unmet prayer needs all around us, but there is also untapped prayer power. Please consider being the one who gives other guys permission to take on the work of prayer and to do it in the most natural way—together!

It is not hard to create a group of guys who are interested in learning to pray. Advertise it something like this: "MEN—Come learn a prayer practice that will work for you." Extend some one-to-one invitations by phone or text message. You may need to say a personal word to some men who trust you: "This way of praying really works for me. I think you'd like it. Come and give it a try." You will need one hour maximum for your first session.

Here are some ideas for teaching *Praying in Black and White* to a group.

❑ You don't need a fancy setup. Provide a *place to sit* and *tables* or *clipboards*. Each participant will need a *black roller-ball or gel pen* and some *paper*. Include a variety of sizes of *plain white paper* and *graph or quadrille paper*. *Rulers, protractors, stencils*, and *compasses* give participants some drawing aids. *Pencils* might reduce the art anxiety for some.

As the presenter you will need an *easel, newsprint, or white paper for the easel* and a *black marker* (thick enough to be seen from where people sit.) You will need a *timer*. An old-fashioned egg timer works well, but you can use your phone or another device. If the timer does not ring or beep at the end, you will also need a *chime or bell*.

❑ Start the session with a prayer or a reading from Scripture. Jesus' passage in Matthew 6:5–15 about prayer is a good option. When you reach the verses of the Lord's Prayer, ask the group to join you in saying it together.

*And when you pray, do not be like the hypocrites, for they love to pray standing in the synagogues and on the street corners to be seen by men. Truly I tell you, they have received their reward in full. But when you pray, go into your room, close the door and pray to your Father, who is unseen. Then your Father, who sees what is done in secret, will reward you. And when you pray, do not keep on babbling like pagans, for they think they will be heard because of their many words. Do not be like them, for your Father knows what you need before you ask him. This, then, is how you should pray: "Our Father in heaven, hallowed be your name, your kingdom come, your will be done on earth as it is in heaven. Give us today our daily bread. Forgive us our debts, as we also have forgiven our debtors. And lead us not into temptation, but deliver us from the evil one." For if you forgive other people when they sin against you, your heavenly Father will also forgive you. But if you do not forgive others their sins, your Father will not forgive your sins.* (NIV)

After you read the passage, tell the group you are going to teach them a way to pray that will help them create a prayer room (or "closet" as the King James Version says) wherever they are.

❑ For a couple of minutes share your experience of *Praying in Black and White*. Explain the idea of prayer without words and stillness through movement.

❑ Give a little remedial drawing class. Ask participants for the names of shapes. As they say them, draw them on the easel—circle, square, hexagon, amoeba, stop sign, team insignia, whatever. . . . You add to their ideas too. Make the shapes large enough to see (six inches, maybe) from where they are sitting. Sloppiness is just fine! After you have drawn the shapes, ask them for ways to add to them. You can use the ideas in chapter 7 to prompt their contributions—dots, lines, arcs. . . . Draw the movements as they say them. Let them know that anything goes in the drawing. Tell them why they will be adding to the shapes and how this replicates the type of praying we sometimes do with words.

❑ On another piece of easel paper, ask them to shout out names for God they could use when they pray. Use chapter 7 to help you. We can use different names for God at different times and in our different prayers. Encourage the participants to choose whichever name feels right for them today.

❑ Now begin really teaching the practice. Refer to chapter 5 to guide you. The plan is to pray and draw in three-minute increments. Tell the group they will be entering a time of quiet. (Avoid talking while drawing.) Ask them to take a big breath and let it out. Do this a couple of times.

Tell the group they will start praying by drawing a shape on the page (on the top or in the middle). In the shape, ask them to write their God name—Holy God, Healing Lord, Jesus, Holy Spirit—whichever name they choose. Tell them, "For three minutes you can add to the shape and draw around it using the ideas above, all the while asking God to be part of the prayer—with words or in silence." Set the timer for three minutes and tell them to begin. When the three minutes are up, ring a chime or a bell. Have everyone take a deep breath. Together say one line of a psalm or another Scripture verse. Write the verse on a piece of paper where everyone can read it. You can use the suggestions in chapter 9 or choose your own verse.

❏ Next tell the group they are going to pray together for about five or six people. The whole group will pray for the same person at the same time. They can use words in their heads if they want (or write them down), but the words aren't necessary. Reemphasize that this is the whole point of *Praying in Black and White*. As we draw, we offer the person into God's care without necessarily knowing what to say. We spend time with them and God by drawing.

❏ Ask one person to tell the whole group the name of someone they would like to pray for and *one* sentence about why. Use just one sentence, because too much information leads to both worry and inappropriate curiosity. You can model this: "I'd like us to pray for John. He's having hip surgery next week." That's enough information. So ask for the name of one person from someone in the group. Then ask the whole group to pray for the named person by drawing a shape and putting the name of the person in it. (Ask for spelling from the person who suggested the name.) For one to three minutes (you can gauge the attention span of the men in the room) everyone will pray for the person by drawing and doodling. Ring the chime or bell at the end of one to three minutes. Have everyone take a deep breath and say the line of Scripture. Then ask for another name. Pray for the new person for the allotted time. Repeat the process as many times as you want. Encourage people to do the entire prayer drawing on one sheet so they can post it somewhere afterward. But if they draw big they are welcome to use more than one sheet. There are not a lot of rules!

❏ For the last three minutes of the time, ask everyone to draw a prayer for someone they personally want to pray for. It's a nice way to end the session.

□ At the end have everyone take a final big breath. Say the line of Scripture once more. You can then say, "And at the end of the prayer, the people all said," and they will usually respond with "Amen."

□ Ask them, "What did you notice while you were praying?"[3] People will respond to this question more easily than, "How do you feel?" or, "Did you like it?" It is a more concrete question.

Conclude the one-hour session by encouraging participants to try the practice on their own for several weeks. Arrange a time for a follow-up session.

# 15.
# Examples

Andy

Here are some other examples of black and white prayers.

## Circular Prayers

This prayer started with two intersecting lines and the name Jesus. Shapes and doodles grew the drawing outward from the center. The intention of the prayer was stillness and time with Jesus.

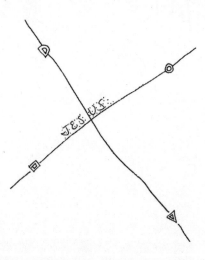

The prayer for Lois began with her name. Eight crooked lines were drawn from the name. All of the later strokes were lines, *U*'s, or *V*'s in different positions.[4] Using just those three movements is a way to construct a circular prayer without much thought. The drawing emerges, but the energy goes into the prayer, not the artwork.

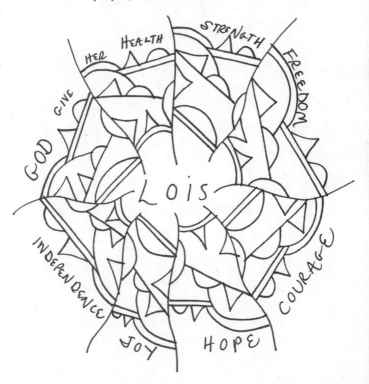

Intercessory Prayers

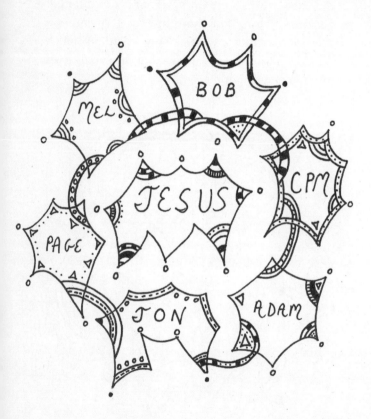

Graph Paper Prayers

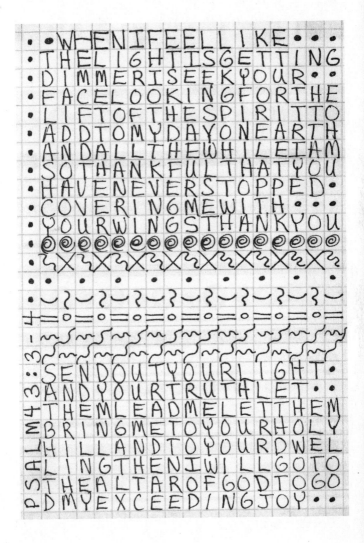

## Family Reunion Prayer

# Final Thoughts

Sybil and Andy

Two words sum up our experience with *Praying in Black and White*—gratitude and amazement. We are grateful and amazed at God's willingness to be accessible to us in the simple tools of pen and paper.

Being attentive to God's presence in our lives is not always easy or natural. *Praying in Black and White* gives us a concrete way to be in touch with the God who permeates our world and is present in our everyday lives in everyday ways.

We hope *Praying in Black and White* will enhance and expand your prayer life too. At the very least, we hope it will set you on a path where you will continue to find new ways to connect with God.

# Acknowledgments

We are thankful for the expertise, creativity, and prayers of the many people who brought this book from a proposal onto paper. Thanks be to God for the following people:

Jon Sweeney, our editor and friend, who gave us lots of artistic leeway and reined us in when necessary;

Lynn Hunter, who read the manuscript and made some wise big-picture and small-detail suggestions;

The design, production, and marketing teams at Paraclete Press for their creative and enthusiastic work—the staff at Paraclete Press seems to love and pray their books into existence;

Bob Edmonson at Paraclete Press for his hawk-eye edits and clarifications;

Constance Denninger and Laura Denninger Schumacher for the contribution of their black and white prayers (pp. 109–111);

Phyllis Tickle, who encourages us again and again to share the prayer practices of *praying in color* and *praying in black and white* with others.

# Notes

Chapter 12

1. The term *mind-mapping* is often attributed to Tony Buzen, a British psychology writer and consultant. The idea of brainstorming has been around for centuries. For years I have collected and collated thoughts, feelings, and information using this method.

Chapter 13

2. For more ideas about finding your personal breath prayer, read Ron DelBene's short but profound book called *The Breath of Life: A Simple Way to Pray*. It is available in hard copy or a downloadable version.

Chapter 14

3. The question "What did you notice?" comes from InterPlay®, "an active, creative way to unlock the wisdom of the body." Visit the website http://www.interplay.org/ for more information.

Chapter 15

4. Our friend Cindy O. came up with the idea of circle drawings (or rosettes) using just *U*'s and *V*'s. Many thanks to her for sharing this helpful and easy way to create a prayer drawing.

# About Paraclete Press

## Who We Are

Paraclete Press is a publisher of books, recordings, and DVDs on Christian spirituality. Our publishing represents a full expression of Christian belief and practice—from Catholic to Evangelical, from Protestant to Orthodox.

We are the publishing arm of the Community of Jesus, an ecumenical monastic community in the Benedictine tradition. As such, we are uniquely positioned in the marketplace without connection to a large corporation and with informal relationships to many branches and denominations of faith.

## What We Are Doing

### Books

Paraclete publishes books that show the richness and depth of what it means to be Christian. Although Benedictine spirituality is at the heart of all that we do, we publish books that reflect the Christian experience across many cultures, time periods, and houses of worship. We publish books that nourish the vibrant life of the church and its people—books about spiritual practice, formation, history, ideas, and customs.

We have several different series, including the best-selling Living Library, Paraclete Essentials, and Paraclete Giants series of classic texts in contemporary

English; A Voice from the Monastery—men and women monastics writing about living a spiritual life today; award-winning literary faith fiction and poetry; and the Active Prayer Series that brings creativity and liveliness to any life of prayer.

## Recordings

From Gregorian chant to contemporary American choral works, our music recordings celebrate sacred choral music through the centuries. Paraclete distributes the recordings of the internationally acclaimed choir Gloriæ Dei Cantores, praised for their "rapt and fathomless spiritual intensity" by *American Record Guide,* and the Gloriæ Dei Cantores Schola, which specializes in the study and performance of Gregorian chant. Paraclete is also the exclusive North American distributor of the recordings of the Monastic Choir of St. Peter's Abbey in Solesmes, France, long considered to be a leading authority on Gregorian chant.

## DVDs

Our DVDs offer spiritual help, healing, and biblical guidance for life issues: grief and loss, marriage, forgiveness, anger management, facing death, and spiritual formation.

Learn more about us at our website:
www.paracletepress.com,
or call us toll-free at 1-800-451-5006.

You may also be interested in

The Jesus Creed Series

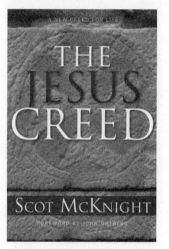

## The Jesus Creed
*Loving God, Loving Others*

SCOT McKNIGHT

ISBN: 978-1-55725-400-9  Paperback, $16.99

*Winner of the 2005 Christianity Today Book Award*

LOVE GOD WITH ALL YOUR HEART, soul, mind, and
strength, but also love others as yourselves. Discover
how the Jesus Creed of love for God and others can
transform your life.

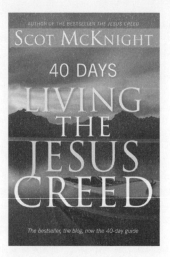

# 40 Days Living the Jesus Creed

### Scot McKnight

ISBN: 978-1-55725-577-8 Paperback, $14.95

"Scot McKnight stirs the treasures of our Lord's life in an engaging fashion. He did so with *The Jesus Creed*, and does so again with *40 Days Living the Jesus Creed*. Make sure this new guide for living is on your shelf." *Max Lucado*

Also in the Active Prayer series

## Praying with the Body
*Bringing the Psalms to Life*

Roy DeLeon

ISBN: 978-1-55725-589-1
Paperback, $16.99

While most books about prayer are meant to be read, this one is an invitation to move in prayer by expressing the Psalms with motion. Benedictine oblate Roy DeLeon guides you with helpful drawings, Scripture texts, and explanations.

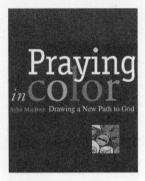